Don't Be Stupid about Money

DontBeStupid.club Answers to Budgeting, Debt, and Other Personal Finance Questions

H. Granville James

ITSUS PRESS

Don't Be Stupid about Money
DontBeStupid.club Answers to Budgeting, Debt, and
Other Personal Finance Questions

Legal Disclaimer: Everything in this book is the opinion of
the author. No responsibility is taken for the application or
use of these thoughts in any specific circumstances.
The reader should *Think for Yourself*.

ISBN: 1530776082
ISBN-13: 978-1530776085

Dedication

The DontBeStupid.club books about money are dedicated to John Bogle.

Mr. Bogle is not stupid about money.

"Saint Jack" stood virtually alone in the wilderness for decades. First millions of dollars, then billions and now trillions of dollars follow his ideas. His ideas, yes. His ideals? Not so much.

"Saint Jack" was not meant as a compliment originally. Legend says it started as an insult.

Among the ideals, there is a simple thesis that investors have no reason to pay high fees to expensive money managers. Investors will do better by paying lower fees for simpler products. It's a well-supported argument using critical thinking at a level we aspire to attain. But it really annoys people whose paychecks depend on fees.

"Saint Jack" is the founder of The Vanguard Group. He is single-handedly responsible for changing an industry, and for saving investors many billions of dollars in fees and expenses. It might even be a trillion by now. The whole industry has lower fees because they have to compete with "Saint Jack". We guess that makes stupid people resort to name calling.

Perhaps our favorite Bogle moment is from an interview on one of those financial shows. We paraphrase here;

Interviewer: You could make a lot more money.
Bogle: How much better would I eat?

Thank you, Saint Jack. Long may you run.

Contents

1.
Let's Begin

EVERYBODY NEEDS MONEY. That's why they call it money.

We borrowed that from Danny DeVito. Or David Mamet if you want to get picky. But without Danny delivering the line, is it worth any money?

Money. Everyone knows about money, right? We all know what money is and we all know we need more of it. There's never enough. Everybody NEEDS money. Why is that? Why is there so much stupidity about money? Maybe... just maybe... we don't know as much as we think. Maybe we're all just a little bit stupid. Maybe we should take a closer look.

Follow the Money is one of our fundamental principles. Money is so important it must always be considered to avoid being stupid. (see DontBeStupid.club for a detailed look at our critical thinking principles. In this book, the principles will be in *italics* to identify them.)

But you can't *Follow the Money* if you don't know what to look for. And you can't accumulate or guard YOUR money if you don't understand it. This is not another one of those "do these ten things and you will be rich" books. When you finish this book, you will be able to choose your own ten things, and hopefully more. It will take a little effort, but we will make it as easy as possible. It's probably easier than you think.

Money. Birds don't care about it. Dogs, fish, trees, gravity, Jupiter, nothing else in the universe cares about money except us. Money is not a part of nature. Humans invented money.

Money is the lifeblood of human civilization. It makes the world go 'round. And it's been doing that since the first time humans traded by mutual agreement instead of killing each other to get something.

(Imagine being the first one to figure that out; it's better to make a trade and keep the other guy alive... maybe we can even trade again tomorrow. How brilliant was the one who thought of that? And how did you explain it to the other guy?)

YOUR money. Your personal finances, savings, nest egg, bankroll, investments and on and on. Whatever name it goes by, and we call it many different names, we spend our life trying to accumulate money. Why?

And everyone else spends their life trying to take your money away from you. That's the most fundamental thing about your money. Everyone else wants it. And we all better be happy about that, because if they stop wanting it then our money isn't worth much.

There is more stupidity in the universe of money, spending it, saving it and investing it, than any other area we encounter regularly. And that's probably because getting your money is the purest expression of human motivation that exists. Humans pursue money with more intensity than anything else. The only thing that even comes close is getting laid, sometimes.

And now that we mention it, the possibility of getting laid is used to extract more money from humans than any other advertising method. Combining the two, sex and money, is the ultimate way to make people get stupid. Add a little booze and you've got... a nightclub! The ultimate money extraction machine. But we digress, let's get back on track.

Buy a home. Spend as much on it as you can qualify to spend. And a car too. More than one so you can look cool and also drop the kids at school. Just pay the interest. Pay the fees. Whatever you do, you must do something so you are spending your money.

And not just your own money, you need to spend more, you need to borrow too. You can't be sane if you are not borrowing money like everyone else. Someone who doesn't borrow is just a whacko. But keep your credit score high, because if you're paying an extra quarter point interest on your debts, well then, you're a failure.

Don't Be Stupid. It's all mapped and planned out so you can never run out of ways to spend your money. We live in the ultimate all-you-can-eat buffet of money sucking choices. Maybe we should try and break the cycle. Maybe we all should do some critical thinking here.

Maybe we can get a little less stupid about money.

2.
What is Money?

SALT HAS BEEN MONEY, wheat, gold, silver, beads, cigarettes, bullets... So what is really money anyway?

Define the Target. Money is anything people accept as having an agreed value so they can make trades using it. Money is a **substitute** for something of real value. Money is what someone will accept in trade for their valuable goods or services, because they know they can use that money to get something else they want. Money's only value is in what else you can get for it. If you have everything you want, then money has no value for you.

We want to repeat that because it's a fundamental point about money that most people miss. If there's nothing you want to buy, then money has no value for you. Money is only worth what you purchase with it. Buy nothing and money is worthless.

This leads to the first fundamental conclusion we can reach about money. The less we want to buy, the less important money becomes. If we want to buy less, then maybe we are already wealthier than we thought... we might even be rich already! And that's not some "new age" nonsense. It's just the definition of money. What can we buy with it? And how much is that really worth to us? Not every culture on earth is based on buying as much as you possibly can. How much is enough?

Now, you will find raging arguments among theorists out there over exactly what is money. People will argue about whether this or that commodity (like gold) is "money", or can any commodity even be money at all, or can "money" only be something used to substitute for commodities, or what happens if a commodity becomes money, or… Who cares! If beads can be traded for what I want today, then beads are my money today.

Dwelling on irrelevant distinctions violates our *Don't Be Distracted* principle. Names and changing naming conventions distract us from what is really important. If the distinction doesn't change the answer we seek, then it's irrelevant.

Money is whatever you can use to buy something today. You are probably carrying several different kinds of money right now.

And money is always changing. This concept is very important to remember. Today's money is not tomorrow's money. It was beads today, but maybe it will be salt next year. Even with the same name, money is always changing. A US Dollar today is quite a bit different from the US Dollar of 100 years ago. Both are money, but *Don't Be Distracted* by the name. Even though both say "one dollar", they are not the same thing. You could buy a lot more with "one dollar" 100 years ago. And if you have a 1924 silver coin that says "one dollar" on it, well, you'd be crazy to spend it like it was one dollar.

Anything can be money. All it takes is people agreeing on it. Of course, the more people who agree, the more convenient it becomes to use something as money. And when enough people agree, they will start doing anything to get it. When you see a lot of people chasing something, willing to fight or even kill over it, start thinking of that "something" as money. Governments issue most money, and try to control it, but really it's up to the people to agree on its value.

A little side story to make that point clearer. As we write this, there are over 100 known community currencies in the USA. Most are irrelevant but a few are actually viable. People use their local currency to buy and sell goods just the same as they would official US Dollars. That local currency is real money anywhere it's traded, and will continue as long as the people using it agree on its value.

Another good example is Bitcoin, which is real money today too. And governments pretty much hate it.

The opposite is also true. Many governments have "money" that nobody wants. It doesn't start out that way, but it ends up that way. And the people holding that "money" get screwed. It's not money any more, but nobody told them that while they were chasing it. Those people didn't understand how money changes.

Perhaps the most entertaining example is the old Zimbabwe dollar. You can buy their 100 Trillion Dollar bill, yes $100 Trillion, for about $50 U.S. Dollars today. It's a gag gift now, not "real" money any more, but at one time the people of Zimbabwe were told to accept it in trade for their goods and services. And that's a shame for those patriots who believed their government. Anyone who didn't ultimately burn one for fuel can trade it today for about $50 US. It's also a reminder of government stupidity when it comes to money.

The point is this: governments tell you what they want you to believe about money. Governments do not always tell you the truth about money. In fact, *Follow the Money*. Frequently it's in a government's best interest to lie about money. You are far better off to *Think for Yourself*. Don't Be Stupid!

As we write this book, US Dollars are the world's most commonly accepted money. It's the majority among the world's reserve currencies, meaning it's the one most people in the world want to hold and hold the most of. .

Now please don't get all patriotic about your local currency. We intend no disrespect. There are countries better at actually making money than the USA. (If you are not in AWE of the German economy, well, you are stupid.) We are not talking about economies here; we are talking about money as defined above. What do people agree to accept in trade for goods and services? And the most widely accepted money in the world today is the US dollar.

We are not going to talk much about "strong" and "weak" currency here. When you hear people talk about "exchange rates" or "floating exchanges" or similar jargon, it's just a statement of what one country's currency is worth compared to another. Meaning right now. It changes tomorrow or even a few minutes from now. Money is always changing for anyone accepting their government's definition of their national currency as their money.

Learn from History. A brief history lesson here for

context. About 100 years ago, money was pegged to gold and silver. If you issued paper "money", you had gold or silver to back it up or no one accepted it. The world accepted these precious metals as money. And a government's paper currency just promised they had that metal and would deliver it on demand. If that were still true today, there never would have been a Zimbabwe 100 Trillion Dollar note. Too bad for the people in Zimbabwe who accepted their government's definition of money.

Today there is nothing backing up national currencies. There is no promise to deliver gold or silver or anything else tangible. The only promise is you can use the currency to make purchases in the country that issued it. There is no value guaranteed.

In reality, US dollars are just pretty pieces of paper. But everyone agrees on their value in the moment and uses them to exchange value, to trade with each other. Right now US Dollars are the most commonly accepted money in the world, and the money everyone else's money is measured against. Euros are also worldwide money. After that, it gets a little murky. All patriots will feel their country's currency is good, and some are more accepted than others, but Dollars or Euros pretty much ends the discussion wherever you may be on earth. Today.

"Today" is an important concept. When thinking about money, it's useful to remember that all paper money has failed and become worthless sooner or later. Odds are good that someday, sooner or later, the USA paper will not look so pretty either. As we mentioned already, the $1 bill with George on it, it's not nearly as pretty as it was

100 years ago.

As we write this book, the USA and Eurozone are pursuing inflation. They're doing just about anything they can to cause a little inflation. Inflation means prices go up, so your currency buys less. This is good for governments in debt, and for people who understand money trading enough to profit from inflation. It is not good for the people accepting that same money for their goods or services.

The official goal in the USA is 2% annual inflation. *There Will Be Math*. If the USA hits its goal, the half-life of a dollar is 36 years. Work it out for yourself if you want, but we did it for you. 36 years from now the dollar will buy half of what it does today. I guess it's good to have goals... but Don't Be Stupid. Money is always changing. Always know what you can buy, because that's all money is worth.

The DontBeStupid.club Summary :

- Money is anything of agreed value between the parties using it to trade.

- Governments try to control what their citizens use as money.

- For now, US Dollars are the world's most commonly accepted money.

- Money is always changing.

3.
Programmed to Spend

THE MONEY GAME traps us before we know any better. And the game is fixed so we lose. If we do everything as expected and all laid out for us as "normal", we end up stressed out and in debt. We have to start from this principle: *Open Mind*. We have to see how the money game screws us so we're willing and able to fight back.

There is a path laid out and we are programmed to follow it. The money game is set up to convince us to spend every dollar we have, plus borrow more and spend that too. The programming starts before we have a chance to think about it. You cannot avoid it. It starts when you are too young to know about critical thinking. And it's reinforced with messaging that continues for the rest of your life. We have to challenge it.

You get caught up in the whole saving-for-college thing before you even know you want to go to college. Parents are advised to start a 529 plan when you're born. And often they cannot afford it, because, well come on, being new young parents doesn't exactly mean you're in your peak saving years. It's not the right time for investing, but no one tells them that.

And as soon as you're old enough to understand what's going on, you know about payments. House payments and car payments, and whatever other debts are sucking money from your parents. And then pretty soon you know about saving for school. And then you take a student loan for whatever amount you didn't manage to save, because by then you know payments are just a "normal" part of life. You'll get a credit card when you go to college too. Go ahead and spend more money you don't have, and pay it back later. With interest. This is all just part of a normal life. Right?

Don't Be Stupid. *Think for Yourself*. This is not normal. This is conditioned behavior. It's bad for you. And you can choose to step off this path.

To break a conditioned behavior pattern requires a conscious effort. You have to make a decision not to keep doing what's been easy, stop doing what you've been programmed to do. With just a little effort to break out of the programming now, the rest of your life can be much easier. For a little effort today you get payback for a lifetime. Breaking this programmed life cycle is a great investment. We did it. We know.

How do we get started?

There Will Be Math. Starting right now, stop for just a moment anytime you are going to spend money and ask why? Let's start with this book. Why buy it? Hopefully, it's because you expected to gain more than a few bucks worth of information about money. (We hope we deliver!)

Think about your day's spending when you sit down in the evening. It's fascinating dinner conversation... Were you hungry? Great reason to buy food. Love your daily latte? Great reason to visit Starbucks. Buying those designer shoes today? Maybe. Maybe not. Why did you really buy them? Only you know. But take the time to be aware of the reason. Don't be just another programmed spender. Don't Be Stupid.

Thinking about taking a car loan? Why would you do that? It's stupid. You might as well know that right now. Taking a car loan is stupid. There is always a better financial alternative. If you're in the habit of stopping for a moment to think about why you are spending, you will stop this type of spending before making the mistake. Programmed spenders do not stop to think, they just spend. You can consciously choose that a latte is OK, and a car loan is stupid. That is how you break the programming. You must know why you spend before you spend.

So why do people think it's OK to finance a car? Nobody who understands money recommends financing a depreciating asset. You just leverage a loss into a greater loss.

Define the Target. Depreciating – Diminishing in value over time.

Define the Target. Leverage – Use borrowed capital expecting to increase profits.

Cars go down in value from the moment you start driving them. And it's just stupid to borrow money when only a loss can be expected.

So why is it just part of life to finance a car? *Follow the Money.* Do you think $10 billion in annual advertising has anything to do with it? Let me pose another question. If it's such a good idea, do you think $10 billion in annual advertising would be necessary? You are being programmed to spend. All you have to do to break out is say "No" and *Think for Yourself.*

The monetization of all the "free" social media platforms is accomplished by selling advertising. You get the service for free, but you are being programmed to spend while you're using it. You don't pay to use Facebook. But you see plenty of advertising, tailored and targeted right at you. Facebook collects over $20 billion in revenue because they can promise advertisers that you will see their programming.

This sounds obvious, doesn't it? We were born into a world flooded with advertising. It seems as normal to click through a pop-up ad as it does to breathe. And everyone's first reaction is "Not me. I'm not programmed." To which we say, "Prove It". How much stupid spending have you done? It's impossible to live in a world that constantly barrages you with bullshit and not get a little bit dirty. Use critical thinking as a shield. Reject the programming.

Respect Nature. Not everyone on earth suffers with this programmed-to-spend problem. There are still some people who are not born into a consumption-driven madhouse. Not yet anyway. But the contamination is spreading. When we hear someone use the term "emerging market" or "developing economy" all we see are sharks circling. (Financial hegemony is another book we'd enjoy writing. Best tweet we ever read: "My new IPAD display is so good I can see the tears of the child who made it.")

For now, you can look around at places on earth where people spend relatively little money and yet somehow they manage to lead very happy lives. In fact, if you believe the United Nations, about 65 countries have gotten happier over the past 10 years, while the USA and the UK went the other way, getting more unhappy. Spending is up, and happiness is down.

So money didn't buy happiness. *Think for Yourself*. Realizing that happiness has nothing to do with how much you buy, this might feel pretty weird at first. Like waking up after surgery, or coming out of a drug-induced haze. You've been programmed with an endless barrage of advertising. Just keep buying, and you will be happier, sexier, successful and an all-around better human being. But it's not working.

Then you realize it's just bullshit from people trying to squeeze money out of you. And hopefully, you get pissed off. Because then you are home free. Instead of the seductive messaging, we hear liars trying to steal from us. It makes us mad, and we ignore them. *Don't Be Distracted*. You know what? It turns out we know what we want without anyone else telling us. The path to happiness is much clearer without everyone else's message distracting us. And that is when you are really free of the drug.

Spending is not part of human nature. It's just part of a game that pays off for the wrong people. It's clear money does not buy happiness, just more stuff. Reject the programming! Let's all think about our spending critically.

The DontBeStupid.club Summary :

- We are programmed to spend starting from before we can stop it.
- Relentless advertising tries hard to keep the

programming going.

- We must defend ourselves.

- Not everyone spends like we do. It's not part of human nature.

- Spending does not correlate with happiness. We can choose to stop.

4.
Credit? DEBT!

IF MONEY IS the lifeblood of civilization, then credit is the leech on our neck.

Credit sounds like something good, doesn't it? You get Credit! *Don't Be Distracted*. It's just another case of using a different name to make it sound better. No one really has credit; we have debt.

Define the Target. Credit – The ability to obtain goods or services before payment, based on a promise for payment at a later date.

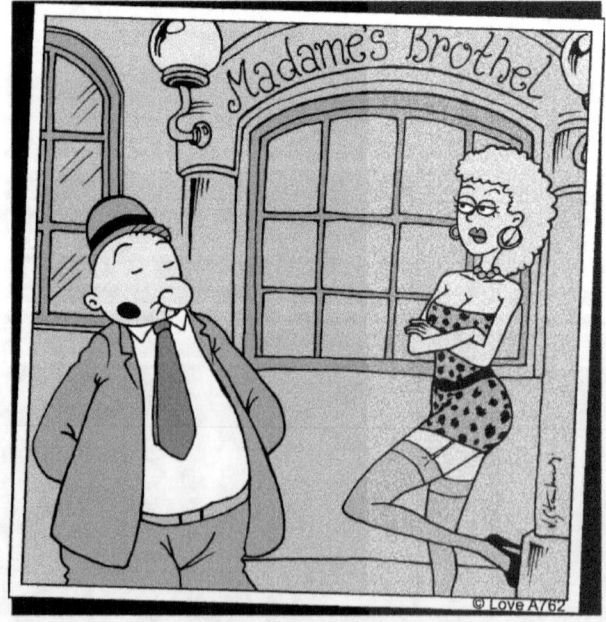

Snapshots at jasonlove.com

"I'll gladly pay you Tuesday…"

But that's not really what a "credit" sale is today, is it? You don't promise to pay next week, and then walk in and pay for the purchase 7 days later, do you? That's what credit really was back when such a thing really existed. "You have credit" is something different today. It's a sales pitch. And it's not even true.

You have no "credit" with the seller. There's just a willingness to accept your credit cards. Your credit card is accepted for the purchase, not your credit. You just have a card. And the card issuer pays the merchant right away the same as if you just paid. No credit, the merchant got paid. And you now have a debt to the card issuer. With a price. You pay the card issuer interest on your debt. And they get a very high return on their loan to you for as long as they hold your debt.

Define the Target. Debt – Money owed or due. Total household debt in the USA alone is over $10 trillion. That's 10 TRILLION dollars. Just in the USA. Europe has more. In the USA, credit card debt alone is over $700 billion. Home mortgages, car loans, and student loans add up to the bulk of the remainder. Borrowers pay a cost for having a debt, usually called interest.

Define the Target. Interest – Money paid for the delay in repaying a debt. It's a very simple arrangement. You borrow money from someone and they charge you a price for the use of their money. The interest rate is your cost to borrow, and it's usually stated as a percentage. Although interest rates are most commonly stated as annually, rates stated for shorter periods are very common and usually misleading.

There Will Be Math. If you pay 2% per week, you are

really paying over 100% interest in the more commonly accepted way of stating that cost, which is annual interest. The weekly number is just giving it another name to distract you. *Don't Be Distracted*. You're paying 100% interest.

We're amazed at "0% interest" offers for balance transfers that are accompanied by a 3 or 4% fee to make the transfer. That's not zero percent interest. That's stupid. *Don't Be Distracted.* None of us is stupid enough to believe we get money for free. Well, maybe we are that stupid sometimes. It's a tempting thought. But why would anyone give us money for free? You don't really think you're getting zero percent financing on that new car, do you?

There Will Be Math. The average rate on credit card debt is over 15% annually. On credit cards alone, lenders are collecting over $105 billion dollars of interest. They collect that profit every year.

Other types of debt have lower interest rates, like mortgages or student loans. But even at an average of 5% interest, there's another $450 billion of interest paid. Annually. Every year. There are also fees and penalties. They are just different names for what it costs you to borrow money. *Don't Be Distracted*. All of it is what it costs you to borrow money. Consider it all part of your interest expense.

Follow the Money. Getting us into debt, also known as lending, is a VERY big business. The incentive to keep us borrowing is so big it's difficult to comprehend the number. Let's put it this way. If we stacked these dollars of debt up, on top of each other like in a cash drawer, that stack would reach to the moon and back. Twice. For the USA alone. Try to get a rubber band around that stack.

No surprise then, the easiest way to get money is to borrow it. You don't have to work. Borrowing is easy. And there's a reason for that. It's profitable for the lenders. Anyone who wants a credit card can find one. Want to buy a car? There's a cheap loan for that. Want a house? There's a mortgage, even cheaper than a car loan. Need money until next payday? There are loan centers for that too.

Why is it so easy to borrow? Well, we explained it already but when challenging a sacred cow, it needs more emphasis. *Define the Target.* Sacred Cow - An idea or belief held to be above criticism. Borrowing is just accepted as a fact of life today. Our suggestion that this might not be "normal" is going to sound a bit weird.

But *Follow the Money.* The reason it's so easy to borrow is that lenders make a fortune. Lenders make a lot of MONEY from our borrowing, even on what appear to be the cheapest loans. And they do not even have to produce a product. We pay them interest just to use something already there. We're just borrowing it.

The only time it's hard to borrow is when you have too much debt already. If you are turned down for a loan, say a sincere "thank you" and take it as a warning sign. It's like the bartender telling you that you've had enough to drink. And the hangover from debt lasts a lot longer. Lenders will do everything they can to make more money from you. The only reason they will not lend even more to you is because at some point they believe you cannot pay for it.

Think for Yourself. We must think about debt critically and reach a different conclusion from that of the majority. Where all this stupidity really begins is by accepting the idea that borrowing is OK in the first place. It's not. Borrowing is stupid. We are trained to borrow from such an early age we really have no choice in the matter. We're hooked by the drug dealers before we know any better. Think "student loan" here if you want. And thank mom and dad for protecting you against that one... or not! But now we're older and smarter. We need to make critical thinking choices about debts and get off the drug.

We are all conditioned to be stupid. Purchases like cars, houses, appliances, TV's and home improvements are routinely sold based on the monthly payment. But for us, *There Will Be Math*. When we buy something with payments, our real cost is the total of the payments. And we add them up. That car does not cost $399 per month. If the loan is for 72 months, the car costs $28,728 plus anything else you pay at time of delivery. We don't care if they name it "zero percent interest" or not. We are going to compare our real cost here to the competition elsewhere and make the best choice.

But really, we don't want payments at all. Debt preys on our desire to have something right now. Instant gratification today. But the debt hangover lasts too long. Anytime we use the discipline to pay as you go, just buy and enjoy what we can really afford today, then we save a ton of money on borrowing costs. There is no hangover from a cash purchase.

There Will Be Math. For an eye-opening exercise, add up all the interest and any other debt expense you pay next month. Just make a little note somewhere every time you pay for borrowed money. Interest on a car, credit card, late fee on a utility bill, bounced check fee, anything you pay to borrow money. Then multiply that by several years and see how far ahead you could be if you stopped borrowing. Add up what the debt really costs. Do this for a while, and very soon that 5-year-old paid off car will look a lot more beautiful than a new one with 60 payments remaining.

The irony of borrowing is this: if you can just avoid the trap, for even a little while, then your savings add up to enough to start making cash purchases without borrowing. And that is when the fun really begins. All the gratification, no debt "hangover", and sellers will even give you a discount for cash. So you save even more money to spend again. That's a lot more fun than having a bunch of credit cards. More rewarding than those rewards points too. We discuss getting out of debt in the following chapters. And you can still get rewards points if you want them.

Let's talk a little about credit scoring. Actually, that's too boring. And stupid. Let's just *Simplify*. Your credit score is important if you borrow money. If you don't borrow money, then who cares? You don't care about a credit score if you don't want to borrow. No, you really don't.

So how much anyone should think about credit scoring has a very simple answer. None. Waste no brain space on it. But to enjoy that simplicity, you have to stop borrowing. That might seem impossible right now. But it's not. Just don't be stupid and you will get there too.

But while working your way out of debt, let's explore some thoughts on credit scores that we hope will reduce your devotion to them.

Please don't believe the BS about needing to use credit to build up your credit score. Yes, your credit score may go up a few points if you borrow some money and pay it back. So what? What is the value in those extra points? *Follow the Money*. The people peddling that "use credit to build credit" stupidity want you to borrow. If you don't borrow, they don't get a paycheck. So borrow to raise your credit score? Yes, that's as stupid as it sounds.

On-time payment history is the most important item in any credit report, not credit use. No landlord is ever going to turn down your lease because you don't have enough debts on your report. And you will never have a bad credit score if you pay bills on time. Do both, pay on time AND have no debt? People will trip over each other trying to lend you money. And you won't need it.

Think for Yourself. Who really benefits from your high credit score? That credit score exists just so they know if you're a good customer for them or not. Are you a good prospect for a sale? Your credit score tells them the answer. It's for their benefit, not yours. Your high credit score is really just a target on your back saying "please sell me some debt". Don't participate in helping them target you. Don't waste time playing their credit score games.

The world of credit scores gets even more stupid. As we discussed, the credit industry wants you to believe your credit score is so important that you will do anything to increase it. But now it's becoming big business to get you to pay to watch over your score too. Credit Monitoring Service? This is unreal. We are asked to pay to help them maintain the tools they use to sell us their products. Can it get any more stupid? Fraud is their problem, not yours. They should pay for our help in preventing it, not the other way around.

We strongly recommend going the opposite direction. Opt out of receiving any credit offers. You don't want more credit offers, and you don't want the credit reporting agencies selling your credit score for their own profit. (The opt-out link is on our website in the Bonus Content section: http://dontbestupid.club/money-bonus-content/) They won't stop completely, but you will get fewer. (You didn't expect them all to just do what you asked, did you?)

Simplify. The sooner you do not borrow, the sooner you can forget about your credit score. And all the noise that comes with it.

We realize the "don't borrow" concept will appear crazy at first. Borrowing is a sacred cow. For most people, borrowing has been part of their life since birth. But *Think for Yourself.* Stop to consider; just a few generations ago, a home mortgage was the only borrowing people did. (Maybe the local bookie, but gambling is another book.) *Learn from History.* Prior to the 1960's, there was no MasterCard, there was no VISA. People actually paid for what they purchased at the time of purchase. They even held mortgage burning parties. Their debt actually got paid off... wow. Debt free. Maybe not so crazy.

Back in the dark ages, people wrote these things called "checks". Checks were this amazing kind of money that gave both buyer and seller something easier to handle than a pile of dollar bills. These paper checks evolved into check cards that later came to be called debit cards. A Debit Card!! What an amazing product for a bank to offer its customers. Just a direct withdrawal from our account. No touching the dirty money. And no debt, just convenient access to the money already ours and in our account.

Follow the Money. But now the future has arrived, and today there's just not enough profit for banks in handling money or making life convenient for their customers. Too much debit card use hurts their profits. Banks need that $100 billion of credit card interest income. How did they ever survive without it!

That's $100 billion on credit card interest we pay every year, just so we can buy things we cannot really afford. We can't pay for it right now, but we can still have it. Isn't that great! And once they get you hooked on buying things you cannot afford, their interest income is secure for as long as you live. It's worse than a drug habit. Even a drug dealer won't sell you more than you can pay for right now.

Avoiding debt is easy. All you have to do is *Think for Yourself*. Once you do, it's easy to live better on less money. Clear thinking, not impaired by the debt drug, results in better housing, transportation, food... all the decisions will be better without debt involved. Think about it. Anything you buy with debt starts off with a big handicap. You don't enjoy that negative feeling accompanying the purchase. Making debt payments is never fun. And it's hard to be happy no matter how nice your house or car is if the payment is stressing you out. We'll talk more about houses and cars later.

We're speaking from experience here. It can be done. Being debt free makes life easy; life is simpler and much more fun. And we're only a little bit crazy.

Time for our reality check. We can't be stupid enough to think everyone will quit borrowing, get off the debt drug and be clean tomorrow. Not everyone can quit "cold-turkey". But remember, Don'tBeStupid.club has a more achievable mission. We just want to make the world a little less stupid.

Try forming this simple habit. When you pick up something to buy, just ask yourself "want or need?". Be honest with yourself, and your spending will go down. And you will also break out from the programmed spending habit. You don't need the distraction of tracking your spending for months or an online budget service, just take control of your own spending. Want or need?

There Will Be Math. The average credit card charges over 15% interest on debt. If every reader reduces their credit card debt by just $1000, that's $150 saved per reader per year. A little less stupid. Mission accomplished. Your goal is to be debt free as soon as possible. But all the baby steps count.

Why do people borrow? *Follow the Money*. Everyone else benefits when we borrow money. The people selling the products, the lenders, the services monitoring your credit, the credit card processing companies... Everyone benefits. Except us. We pay.

Why does anyone REALLY borrow? Only for one reason. Immediate gratification. *Don't Be Distracted*. Let's control our buying impulses; do not borrow. When someone says "credit" hear the real word instead, "DEBT". Get off the drug. Get clean.

The DontBeStupid.club summary:

- Credit is really debt. No one has "credit" today. Just debt.

- We pay a price to have debt. And the industry collecting it is huge. Getting people into debt is a very Big Business.

- We can break the debt cycle by paying as we go. Just treat debt like a bad drug. Kick it. Baby steps are ok. Any progress helps.

- Use "want or need?" to begin control of your own spending decisions.

5.
Budgeting

THIS WHOLE CHAPTER is a lot of math. Easy math, but it's all math. So we're only going to say it once here at the beginning. *There Will Be Math*. Now let's run some numbers.

OK, here it is. The DontBeStupid.club (almost) Universal Flex Budget.

We live a pay-as-you-go life. No debt allowed; therefore, our budget must be derived from our income. *Open Mind*. The Budget dictates what you can buy. You must break away from the prior programming that tells you to buy everything you want. You cannot know what you want yet. It all starts with the budget. Using the budget numbers as your guide, you then want anything they will pay for. Everything else is a non-starter. If you can't pay for it, you don't buy it.

Housing 30%, Food 20%, Transportation 10%, Utilities 10%, Insurances 5%, Phone 5%, Luxuries 5%, Other 5%, Investing 10%

All numbers are after tax because we can only spend the cash we have left after the government takes its cut. And the budget flexes because you can move money between categories easily. In fact, that's the point of the flex budget. It's a starting point.

These allocations are the baseline, and good for between about $40,000 and $100,000 of annual income. Below $40K, we ignore investing and put that toward housing. Over $100K, we push the investing percentage up and everything else down to balance, especially housing and transportation. A nice house and car are great. But we don't need something even better just because we can afford it. We live well, and better as we make more money, but we never just buy as much as we can. Nobody needs as much house or car or other debt as you "qualify for" when making over $100K.

Let's build our example off of someone making $40,000 per year. And we'll assume they net $36,000 take home after-tax income. This is roughly the median income for an individual earner in the USA for 2015.

Define the Target. Median – The value at the midpoint of a set of observed values, such that there are an equal number of observed values above and below it. Median is better than a simple average when talking about income. Unless you've been living under a rock, you know the top 1% make A LOT more money than everyone else. That skews the average too much. In other words, more than half the people make a below average income. But we're distracting ourselves now... if you want to explore median vs average any further refer to the statistics section on our website. But do it later. *Don't Be Distracted* right now.

Build your own example using the percentages above multiplied times your own after-tax income. Just do the math for now, and don't worry about how ugly these numbers might look.

So, for the median wage earner, their take home is $3000 per month. The monthly bills should look like this: Housing $900, Food $600, Transportation $300, Utilities $300, Phone $150, Insurances $150, Luxuries $150, Other $150 and Investing $300. Simple. Now we just have to make it work.

OK, let's do a real life example of making it work. Our starting point is this: the budget tells us what we can buy, not the other way around. Make this adjustment right now. Life does not start with what you want; it starts with what you have available to spend. Your budget will tell you what you should want.

Next step, you work from the biggest expense down. All expenses are not created equal. The biggest have the most impact. You start with getting the big ones right and the lesser ones fall in line.

We start with housing. Our budget tells us we want something for $900 per month. Now, what do we want? Well, we like city life so we're going to use Chicago. And for $900 monthly, we're going to choose a nice studio apartment in the Lincoln Park neighborhood. Housing, done.

Next, $600 per month for food. As long as you're not stupid, you can eat like royalty on this amount. Families of four have this kind of food budget. A single person should be able to visit Starbucks regularly, and have plenty left to spend on wine too. Smart food budgeting begins with cooking occasionally, eating real food always, and not wasting your money on prepared or processed junk food. And REALLY don't waste your money on take out. That's financially stupid and unhealthy to boot. You can eat poorly and drive up your medical costs too with stupid eating.

Transportation is our next biggest expense. Now here some fun will start already thanks to our smart housing choice. We don't need a car if we live in Lincoln Park. Our CTA unlimited ride pass is $100 per month and it takes us everywhere in Chicago. We'll add in another $100 for some Uber or Zipcars, and we're still only spending $200 monthly on transportation. We've got $100 to spare from our transportation budget! So we're going to take that extra and put it into housing; now we're going to take that small one bedroom for $1000 per month. Or maybe we'll stay with the original studio and buy more wine instead? We can decide later. Having $100 extra is a nice problem.

OK, we've just put ourselves into one of Chicago's great neighborhoods, covered our housing, food and transportation costs, and are well within our debt-free budget.

Utilities in our apartment are going to be less than the $300 budget allowance unless we run the A/C with the windows open. Heat and trash pickup is included in our rent, electric will average under $100 even if we don't give a shit about conservation, and the internet connection at $50 will be plenty fast. And please don't say you want cable TV. Don't be stupid. Buy the Amazon Fire TV with HD antenna bundle (see the link at the end of the book) and say goodbye to cable bills forever.

At this point, we might have another $50 per month left over from utilities that we can allocate to something else. Depends on how much conservation we practice. For more wine we will conserve electricity!

Our phone budget is $150 per month. That's pretty straight ahead; not hard to have the current model with unlimited data at that price. But wait, maybe we want to use an older model. If we have a paid off phone, we can get all the usage we need for about $50 per month. Allocate another $100 for wine? We love the flex budget!

Insurances should be easy, as long as you have health insurance through your employer. And it should be way less than the budget. If you do have to buy health coverage, we'll have to take away some of that extra wine and put it toward insurance instead. But find a job that includes your insurance, or else get paid more so you can buy it yourself. In any case, this budget gives you a clear look at the value of that fringe benefit.

The rest of the categories kind of speak for themselves. We think everyone can figure out how to spend $150 on luxuries. "Other" has to cover things that don't come up all the time. Maybe you have to go to the dentist, or have a prescription co-pay, or buy some clothes. You may need to use some of your "luxury" money in the month you decide to buy clothes. Flex between categories to make it work.

Everyone needs to live with their budget for a few months to see how it all flows, where you flex money into and out of, but if it starts from this baseline then you should eventually find the balance that works for you. The point is to understand your spending, and not copy ten things someone else tells you to do.

Investing is the lowest priority but a firmly committed part of the budget. We'll talk in more detail about investing later, but here's the key point for budgeting. Investing comes LAST. Forget all the nonsense you've heard before about saving 10% first. *Follow the Money*. That's BS promoted by people trying to sell you their investments and services. For purposes of budgeting, this 10% is available first for any unexpected expenses. Investing for the future is decidedly optional at this stage. We live in the present.

We have to digress a little here and talk about the value of a dollar. *Think for Yourself*. There is a fundamental flaw in this fallacy that you should save 10% of your income for retirement. The flaw is this: all dollars are not equal. The fewer dollars you have, the more they are worth. Those charts showing if you just start investing young enough then you will have a happy and wealthy retirement 40 years later? Bullshit. They're used to sell you on the investment products. Those charts are wrong. The dollars are not all equal.

Tournament poker players understand this concept very well. With big stacks, their individual chips are not worth as much as those in a small stack. When a big stack bets at a small stack, it's not a fair fight. One of those big stack chips just doesn't mean as much as one from the small stack. Why? Because that's all the chips you get. If you lose them, you're out of the tournament. The big stack has more room to play.

With your budget, the exact same rules apply. If you are living on $40K per year, your dollars are worth more to you than to the guy making $100K per year. It is far easier for the $100K per year earner to set aside 10% for investing. Those dollars don't mean as much to his housing or food. He has more room to play. This is obvious and anyone telling you otherwise deserves to have their motives questioned. Or maybe they're just stupid.

First Things First. Do not save or invest until your dollars are worth a little less than when you started your debt free life. How much less? When you feel no stress associated with it. Today we just want to enjoy living a pay-as-you-go life without adding debt. We must live a good life today, and enjoy it enough to be motivated to invest for tomorrow. Set aside any extra, and if you find yourself stress-free after a few months, go ahead and think about investing what you have set aside.

We see the opposite of this promoted as fact every day, everywhere. Save first, then live your life. It makes us crazy. It's terrible advice. It's 100% self-serving bullshit offered by the people who want to collect fees and expenses from your investments. *Think for Yourself.* Take care of your immediate priorities first and invest for tomorrow when today is secure. Invest when you can afford it, and not before. If anyone really thinks they can make a valid contrary argument, feel free to try. And please play in the next poker tournament we enter...

OK, so now let's have a candid discussion of where we are. We're living in a great neighborhood in a nice studio or small one bedroom. We're eating well, mostly organic, we're regulars at Starbucks and drinking some wine too. We have a good phone streaming unlimited data and we're watching movies like crazy on our Amazon Prime account. Chicago Bears games are free with our HD antenna. Our CTA pass is taking us all over Chicagoland. We're buying a few luxuries or maybe just new socks every month. And NO DEBT. Not too bad for $40K a year.

All of this because we let our available income dictate our budget. Here's what we did not do. We did not buy a house even though we "qualify" for the mortgage. We did not get a bigger apartment that would suck money out of all the other categories. We did not get a car even though we "qualify" to pay $400 per month. And we're not using our credit cards. The only time we'll be in an expensive restaurant is when we've got enough in the bank to cover it with our debit card. Instead of spending like every other programmed drone, we have a debt-free, stress-free life.

Want more? Get over it. The budget tells you what you can want. You don't make enough money to buy more. You can only "qualify" to borrow for more. And that is stupid.

That's how budgeting works. It's not about buying what you want first, and seeing what you have left over later. It's not stressing about the rent due and then counting how many lattes you drink trying to save $10 a week later. It's not about tracking your expenses so you get an idea where your money goes. *Don't be Distracted*. Your budget already tells you where the money must go. And *First Things First*. Every budget starts from what you have available to spend. Your choices are guided by your budget, not the other way around.

We did our example to paint a real life picture. But the point is to make it personal to you. Don't Be Stupid with your money. Do the simple budget we presented and make your life fit what you can afford. If you don't like our priorities, use your own. Move some percentages around. But the final total can never be more than 100%.

Budgeting is simple as long as you get your head straight at the beginning. The budget tells you what you can buy. You do not buy what everyone else tells you to buy. You choose from whatever is available to you within your budget.

And here's what happens in real life. You learn to live on what you earn. Then your earnings increase. But you're already happy. So now you have EXTRA money. What a concept. Budgeting like this really is easy, and once it becomes a habit you can do it on autopilot. (And you don't have to waste money on the next "do these 10 things and get rich" book.)

Remember when setting your budget priorities, housing will be your biggest decision. Overspending on this category will kill everything that follows. Always pay the lowest amount for housing required to keep you content. If you can move that down to 25%, great! Cars are the next biggest potential mistake. Never buy a new car until you really have plenty of money. And try not to buy any car at all; they're expensive. Get just these two priorities right in your budget, and the rest falls into place pretty easily.

By the way, if you believe it's impossible to live on the budget dictated by your income, don't bother skipping latte's trying to make up the difference. The single biggest enhancement you can make to your budget is to get a roommate. Just find someone to share that housing line item on the budget. And the next thing to do is live near your work. Commuting is expensive. Driving costs you around 35 cents per mile even in an economy car. Again, get those two big ones under control and everything else works out pretty easily.

The DontBeStupid.club summary:

- Budgeting is simple math.

- Budgeting starts with how much money you have available.

- Choices are dictated by the budget, not by what you want. You have to want what you can afford to buy.

- Housing and transportation are the two items that matter most. Get them in line and the rest are easier to handle.

- Investing is optional until the money is available without causing stress. Live in the present.

6.
Enhanced Budgeting

NOW THAT WE know the budget is the boss, what happens if we want more than the budget says we can afford? The easy answer for stupid people is to borrow. You want something today but cannot afford it. So you let a lender buy it for you. You still can only spend whatever you bring in, but now the lender just trapped you into spending on payments to them with interest. Their profit is now part of your regular spending. *Don't Be Distracted*. Your income has to match up with spending. Lenders try to make you forget that, but forgetting doesn't make it go away. You can look away before a crash, but it still happens.

The only way to spend more without being stupid is to bring in more. So how do we get more money into the budget? Well, let's start with an Occam's razor type answer. Get a second job. If you want to buy more stuff, work more hours and get more income. Simple. And not unusual either. Some people actually work more so they can buy more. Imagine that.

Is it worth it? Only you can decide. If you match the work required directly to what you buy with it, maybe some of that stuff doesn't seem worth buying anymore? But if you think it's worth it, then it's a well-reasoned decision and not stupid. Borrowing to buy stuff is stupid. Working to buy stuff is a good decision as long as you've thought it through.

An easier way to enhance a budget is to make the existing money buy more. In our budget example, we chose the Lincoln Park neighborhood in Chicago. We chose there to make the point you can live very nicely in a big city even on a single average income. But Lincoln Park does not make anyone's low prices list. *Open Mind*. If you need to make a budget stretch, you would choose somewhere else to live. For example, you can do very nicely in Boise Idaho for 50% less.

You can also look for room rentals in larger houses. Anyone can do this, but we really like it for single persons, and it can also work great for a single parent with a child. Just type room rentals and your city into google. In most cases you'll get some craigslist hits and also some local websites. Look carefully and don't be stupid. There are a lot of bargains out there. Craigslist seems to do a good job with this, lots of listings and pictures.

The dominating items in your budget are housing and transportation. You can enhance any budget by not being stupid with these two, and also by making them important considerations when choosing a job. Let's do some examples. These are real life numbers.

There Will Be Math. You can choose between two jobs, one in San Francisco paying $100,000 per year, and one in Cleveland paying $60,000 per year. No brainer, right? Don't be stupid. To keep it simple, we'll assume you live downtown in both places and don't need a car. In Cleveland, you will have ample housing choices well within your 30% budget. In San Francisco, using only 30% of your budget is going to make housing a problem. Yes, if you work hard you can find something in SF in that price range, but the places you want to live in are about twice what your budget would allow. So you can choose to be poor in San Francisco making $100K per year, or pretty well off in Cleveland making $60K per year.

Let's alter that example to something more common. This is a stupid decision a lot of people make, so let's take a look. You bought a house in the suburbs. And you have a garden and a lawn to mow and life is just peachy. And you drive 15 miles to work every day; it only takes about 25 minutes and you're OK with that. *There Will Be Math*. Assuming your car has no debt, it costs you about 35 cents a mile to drive. That's $10.50 per day, or about $2600 per year to go to work. You have to earn over $3000 before taxes just to pay for your commute. Whatever your salary is, you gave yourself a $3000 pay cut.

Add another 200 miles per month for other driving errands, and now you've got about a $4000 pay cut. Need two cars? Add it all up. When you choose to live in the suburbs, your transportation costs are everywhere. And if you cannot stop yourself from buying the super cool SUV then you're really in trouble.

Want to enhance your budget? Live close to your job. Get rid of one or two cars.

Your other big budget item is food. You can be very smart and enhance your budget, or very stupid and wreck everything. Let's say you spend $10 on take-out

just five times per week. That's not too often considering three meals a day; be honest when you count these up. We picked something pretty typical. That's $50 per week on take out. If you cook at home, you can eliminate all of that. Now don't try arguing you'd spend more to cook at home. That's stupid. You will spend nothing extra, you will be smarter about your food choices and throw less away. Leftovers make great lunches.

Hopefully, you get the idea enough for budgeting purposes; get creative and eat real food. We love beans and rice… tastes much better than a steak dinner with monthly payments on the side.

For budget purposes, we'll leave you to trust your own *Common Sense* here. But check out our food books for more on this. They describe in more detail how we are not stupid about food.

We mentioned a roommate was a great way to enhance a budget. And if you can live happily with someone else, then there is no better way to enhance a budget. You can cut housing down to 15 or 20% and still have a great place to live. And that means you have a lot of money left over. If you can share the food and transportation bills too, then two incomes effectively make you rich. All you have to do is budget correctly.

Our budget example in the previous chapter was based on the median income for one. If you double that number for two people, you have $6000 per month for the budget and you end up with Housing $1800 per month, Food $1200, Transportation $600, and Utilities $600. We'll leave off the rest of the budget for now and those items just go with each individual (No one shares a phone anymore).

Bottom line, two people can live in a very nice place for $1500 per month, and eat well for $800 per month. And the utilities don't go up to anywhere near $600, more likely they will total about $300. So both people save at least $500 back into their budgets as opposed to living alone. Each budget was enhanced more than 15%, plus you're living in a bigger and nicer place too. It helps if you like your roommate. The obvious choice is a good life partner, spouse or whatever.

Want to go for a bigger pot of gold? Add more roommates. This is not as crazy as it sounds. Historically, multiple generations of a family shared the same house. You can do the budget examples if you want, but the math should be clear by now. If you have three or four paychecks contributing to the bills, you get rich fast. Of course, at some point life is about remaining sane and not being rich, so you have to be sure you like your roommates. We're just making budget points here.

The Don't Be Stupid Club summary;

- Enhance your budget by getting a second job. Earning must match spending

- Make your existing budget buy more. Start with a smart housing choice.

- Consider housing and transportation important when choosing a job.

- Sharing expenses enhances a budget considerably.

7.
Home

Follow the Money. Many other people profit when you buy a home, so you are told at every opportunity that buying a home is a great idea. It's stated as a fact of nature and you are expected to just accept it. But *Think for Yourself*. Is it really good for you? Maybe. Maybe not. Buying a home is a very good idea for some people, but it is stupid for a lot of other people.

If you want to buy, then they will qualify you to buy as much home as possible. Sounds fantastic! I qualified for a really big home! *Don't Be Distracted*. Being "qualified" is just a marketing technique used to make you feel better about buying their product. Let's say this more honestly and see how it sounds:

"We will figure out how much we can possibly lend you and still think it's a good deal for us. Once we know how much debt can we possibly sell you, we'll let you buy it from us for the interest rate, points and closing cost prices we set."

Take your time here. Read that again. We will wait. But read it again. Isn't that really what is happening? They will sell you as much debt as they think you can pay back. And they set the price. Lucky us. We qualified!

We hope that sounds bad, because that is exactly the stupidest way to go about buying a home.

Follow the Money. Everyone trying to sell you a home makes money. And selling you as much home as you can qualify to borrow? That is just maximizing their income. Everyone makes a percentage of your deal. There are commissions and fees for every aspect of the deal, the brokers, the lenders, the escrow agent, and the tax man just to name a few. They all have their hands in your pockets when you buy. You are "qualified" to make them as much money as possible. It has nothing to do with what is best for you. *Think for Yourself.* Your best decisions require doing your own analysis.

Get just this one decision right and it can make everything else easier, even cover a lot of smaller mistakes you might make later. But get this one wrong, and it can ruin the rest of your life. If there is one budget item that can help people the most, this one is it. This is the big one, we have to get it right.

The single biggest mistake people make in managing their money is taking on too much debt to buy a home. In general, buying the least amount of house that makes you happy is your best financial choice. This is your biggest expense, and it stays with you for a very long time. For most of us, housing is the single biggest expense in our life.

Our budget has a baseline. Like all guidelines, it's not perfect. But this one is pretty close. Your home expense should be no more than 30% of your income. Rent or buy, it doesn't matter. Once you pass 30% of income for your residence, you will start feeling the pressure in all of your other life needs.

Mortgage lenders will "get you qualified" up to 35 or

even 40% of income. There are calculators everywhere to tell you "how much home you can afford". Who cares! They calculate what's good for the lenders, not you. You don't need a financial calculator. Multiply your take-home pay by 30%. It will give you a better answer. Not better for the lender, and not the answer you might want to hear, but it's a better answer for your financial health.

But *First Things First*. Is buying or renting the right choice?

You have to live somewhere. But is buying a good idea? They told you you're "qualified" up to "whatever" dollars monthly payment. Is borrowing "whatever" they tell you a good idea? Is taking the maximum debt you can qualify for a good idea?

There are fundamental arguments in favor of buying. Rent payments are not building any equity, they're 100% gone to the landlord the day you make them. When you buy, you're building up a little equity as you pay down the mortgage. And the home may go up in value, so if you own it then that added value is yours. And interest expense on a mortgage might be tax deductible. All good reasons to buy.

There are fundamental arguments against buying. You may want to move and selling a home is expensive; there are closing costs and interest expense to pay on a mortgage debt; the home may go down in value; you have to make the down payment in cash right now; and you will have to pay the property taxes and insurance and maintenance on the property as well as any unexpected problems like roof leaks. These are all good reasons to rent.

Simplify. If you plan to move in the next five years, or just want to feel free to move on short notice, then buying is a bad decision. The reason is that all the expenses associated with buying, the expenses in getting a mortgage loan, the broker commissions, the escrow fees, the taxes, the inspections... all the expenses associated with a purchase are paid at the start, right when you buy. If you move too soon after buying, then you've wasted a whole lot of money on needless expenses. Plus, you'll pay more expenses to sell, like another broker commission, transfer taxes, etc.

Assuming you want to stay put for a while, meaning you're going to live there more than five years, then *There Will Be Math*. We have to do a rent vs. buy analysis.

You have to live somewhere. You can buy or rent. What will each one cost? Open a new Excel sheet or take a piece of paper and use a pencil. Make two columns, one "Rent" and the other "Buy". Put the monthly expenses for each choice in the appropriate column. Now total. Compare. And now you've completed your rent vs. buy analysis. Congratulations. Too easy? OK let's do a real example.

The rent number is easy to get. Let's say the rent costs $1200 per month. Be sure and know what the rent includes. Here let's assume it includes heat, trash pickup, water, sewer, exterior maintenance and HOA fees. You pay your own electric and internet fees.

Now we must do a little work to fill in the "Buy" column. Start with the mortgage payment. Let's use a $250,000 mortgage for 30 years at 4.5%. The payment is about

$1266 per month.

Actually, if you want to *Simplify* here, we would not object too strongly. Just comparing the mortgage payment to the rent payment frequently may give you enough information to make a decent decision. In this example, if $1200 is the maximum your budget allows, then there's no way buying will be smart. The mortgage payment is already too high, and we're not done adding costs to this column.

But to be more informed, let's put in a little more effort. Let's look at a less expensive house with a $150,000 mortgage. Yes, we know you qualify for more. But now we know that is stupid useless information, right? The mortgage payment on $150,000 is $760 per month. Now we've got something worth analyzing!

You see this acronym a lot, PITI. That's Principle, Interest, Taxes and Insurance. For most people, that's what they really think of as their "mortgage payment". They make their payment, and the servicer takes care of dividing it up among the PITI. We already know the $150,000 mortgage costs $760 per month. Taxes vary widely depending on where you are, but let's add $200 per month here as a reasonable example. And $75 per month is a reasonable insurance estimate. So our PITI total is $1,035.

Some of the mortgage payment will be principal and some will be interest. The part of your payment that is principal pays down the mortgage, so you owe less debt on the house with each payment. That's like savings, not really an expense. And if your government subsidizes home buying, then you get a tax deduction for the interest expense. That little part of that interest expense you get back at tax time is not really an expense either. Property taxes are frequently tax deductible too. These items are like a rebate, so we do not use the full PITI as the buy expense, we reduce it by the rebates. It's OK to estimate a little here. You don't have to know your exact tax benefit. If in doubt, just take 15% of the interest and taxes for an estimate of your tax rebate. For our example we're going to credit $140 per month back as a tax rebate reducing buying expense.

What about HOA fees? Many homes are in associations with fees for the common areas. Normally these are included in a rent payment. But if you own the place, then you pay them directly to the homeowner's association. You have to add HOA fees into your "buy" column. We're going to use $100 per month here.

Also add into the cost of owning any other expenses that would not be there if you rented. Does rent include any utility costs that an owner pays? Our rental example includes water, sewer, garbage pickup, and exterior maintenance like landscaping costs, etc. We better add $150 per month back into the cost of buying column to cover all those. And we have to reserve a little for unscheduled repairs that a landlord would cover. A/C unit breaks, roof leaks, etc. Let's say $50 per month for repairs.

So now our cost of buying column adds up to $1,195.

You also have to put up the down payment when buying. Whatever that amount is, it's money that could have been used for something else. What potential return on that money are you giving up? If you would just blow it on stuff with no investment value, then you can ignore this item. But for our example, let's say it's sitting in a savings account earning $5 per month in interest. We lose that $5 per month interest so that makes our buy column costs total a nice round number of $1,200.

But if you have 15% credit card debt to pay down, be sure and include the cost of that debt here. You could pay off that other debt instead of using your cash as down payment to get more debt. If you have $20,000 to use for a down payment, but have $20,000 in credit card debt, that $20,000 can earn 15% forever by paying off the credit card. That would mean $250 per month more cost attached to the buying column.

When you're done making this as precise as you think is valuable, total the two columns and take a look. Everyone's circumstance is different. But in general, buying is rarely the "no-brainer" everyone wants you to think. In fact, this is usually a close decision.

In our example, assuming no better use for the down payment money, we came up with each of them costing $1200. Yes, we did that on purpose. But it is clear that the mortgage payment looked pretty low when we started at $760 per month, and it still turns out to be a very close decision versus renting. *Don't Be Distracted*. All those advertisements that say "own from $750 per month" are bullshit. Do your own analysis and get the right answer.

Two factors can tip a close decision one way or the other. First, sometimes it just feels better to own your place. It's yours. You can knock a hole in the wall if you want to. Also, generally speaking, homes increase in value. This is not always true, and it becomes less true the shorter the time horizon. But if you are getting a 30-year mortgage, and plan to stay put and pay it off, then the odds are good your home will be worth more at the end than when you started.

Those added bonuses are usually enough to make owning a home worth the cost of borrowing if everything else is a close decision. But only if it's a close decision.

By the way, the fact homes go up a little in value leads many people to call them a good investment. In general, that is not true. Usually, there are better uses for the money. The investment value of a home comes from the fact you are going to live somewhere for the next 30 years anyway, so you might as well get some value out of it. The principal pay-down in a mortgage payment is a forced savings. Whatever value you realize, it's more than if you'd just paid rent and blown the rest on wine and partying for those 30 years. If you are paying off a mortgage without really thinking about it for 30 years, that is good and you should feel very happy about it when burning your mortgage. But in a fundamental analysis, houses do not come out very well when compared straight up to other investments.

Home mortgage interest is a special kind of debt expense. Depending on where you live, the interest expense may be subsidized by a tax deduction from your government.

Define the Target. Tax Deduction - An expense amount subtracted from gross income prior to computing the tax on said income.

For this discussion, let's assume you have a mortgage and also have a little money to invest. Is paying down the mortgage your best choice?

Well, debt is debt. And we already know you are better off without debt. The only added complication here is a tax deduction for mortgage interest. Let's explore that tax break on mortgage interest a little more.

One of the more stupid things we hear people say all the time is they can't pay off their mortgage because they need the tax deduction. Need it?

There Will Be Math. A tax deduction is worth exactly what it saves in taxes. You don't benefit 100%. You never benefit 100%. The benefit is just the tax percentage of the total expense. For example, if you pay 30% income tax, then a $10,000 tax deduction is worth $3,000 to you. Yes, you will save $3000 on your taxes. But you're still out the other $7,000. The deduction made the $10,000 expense into a $7,000 expense because you got $3,000 back on your taxes. That's all. It didn't make it free.

Does anybody really "need" that expense? The most any tax deduction can do is reduce the impact of an expense. If you must have interest expense on a debt, then a tax deduction makes it a little less painful. But it does not make it something good.

Think of it this way. You run your head into a brick wall at 10 MPH. But with the tax deduction, you hit the wall at only 7 MPH. Much better. But do you need it?

It might be better to pay off the debt and not hit the wall in the first place. *Simplify.* At this writing, the vast majority of USA households pay less than 20% income tax. We feel comfortable in saying forget the tax deduction and pay down the debt. There will be no better investment than paying off the debt. Start with all non-deductible debt first like credit cards, etc. Then pay down home mortgage debt when it is the only debt remaining.

Even for those in higher tax brackets, the evaluation is still between the alternate use of the money and paying down debt. Which will yield a better return?

There is a pervasive tendency to look at the money saved on taxes because you paid mortgage interest. But that's just a tax deduction; you get back a piece of the total interest expense. *There Will Be Math*. If you are in a 20% incremental tax bracket, then you get back 20% of the interest you paid at tax time. But if you paid off the debt, you'd have no interest expense at all.

Should you pay down mortgage debt? That depends. Do you have somewhere better to invest the money? Remember, paying down debt is risk-free so your return is guaranteed. But if you can earn enough more, then "somewhere better" might be the better investment. Some people argue the gains on the S&P 500 index are a better investment than paying down mortgage debt. Maybe. We'd have to see their tax return and gauge their appetite for risk. Anyone who claims a single answer is right is just being stupid. But when in doubt, you are never wrong to pay down debt. It is never a stupid decision.

And if you spend your tax deduction on drinking more expensive wine, for example, then the better investment is definitely paying down the mortgage no matter how high your tax bracket.

As a closing example of home ownership done right, let's look at one of the richest homeowners in the world.

Warren Buffet has lived in the same house for more than 50 years. One of the richest guys in the world, same house, 50 years. He's added on a few times and made it nicer over the years. Actually, from the pictures we've seen, it looks like a fantastic house. And Warren deserves it.

But that house was cheap when he bought it, not even the median priced house for the area. Kind of makes sense Warren Buffett would buy a "fixer-upper" doesn't it? Something tells us he wasn't interested in what he "qualified" for. He made that house decision using our *Think for Yourself* principle. But Warren has been using that principle since long before we made it one of ours. He's never let anyone sell him as much debt as they could "qualify" for him to buy.

The DontBeStupid.club summary:

- Buying a home is not always the best decision, whether you "qualify" or not has nothing to do with it.

- The longer your time horizon, the more likely buying is a good idea. If you think you will move in the next five years or just need flexibility, then buying is usually stupid.

- Don't let other people tell you how much debt to accept. "Qualifying" is only for their benefit.

- There is one debt that might be worth keeping for a while, and that is a home mortgage. But not always.

8.
Car

FOR MANY PEOPLE, the next biggest expense after a home mortgage is car payments.

The discussion of car payments only needs the same concepts we've covered in preceding chapters. But it's necessary to re-emphasize them specifically for car payments. They have impact similarities to house payments; they are relatively large and go on for a long time. And a bad car buying decision can make your life miserable for many years. Yet for most people, it's an automatic choice. Of course you borrow money and have car payments. We love to buy cars!

Buying a car on payments is just taking on debt. All of our previous discussion on the debt applies. There is more emotion attached to a car, and a lot more advertising to convince you it's something special. Usually it's sexy and not even subtle about it. But it's not really sexy. It's just debt. And debt has caused more than one case of impotence. So *Follow the Money* again. Who benefits when you take on debt to buy a car? Should you really buy as much car as your payment can qualify? Don't Be Stupid.

How about this radical idea? Debt is bad. You should not have any car payments at all. None. If you are making your best financial decision, then your car payment should be zero. If you want to accumulate money, the single best strategy you can adopt is to never have a car payment again. Pay cash when you buy a car. And use alternate transportation until you can do so.

What is the purpose of a car? Are you going to make money with it? If you're going to make money with the vehicle then maybe, just maybe, you might be able to justify some debt. But for most people, we're just buying a car to get around; get to work, the store, drop off the kids, etc. How much car do we really need? Do we need one at all? This is where we get stupid.

Don't Be Distracted. Incredible sums of money are spent on selling us cars. Roughly 15 million new cars are sold in the USA alone every year. It's a purchase we are conditioned to make by endless exposure to compelling emotional messages.

For many people, owning any car at all is a bad financial idea. If you live in an urban area, visit walkscore.com and check out your neighborhood. If you see a score over 80, you are probably wasting money owning any car at all. Seriously, that sounds crazy at first, but *There Will Be Math*. Add up all the costs of owning a car; don't forget maintenance, insurance and parking. If you live in a walkable neighborhood, you likely will determine you'd never spend that much on alternate transportation whenever needed.

As we write this, an unlimited pass on CTA, the Chicago Transit Authority, is $100 per month. In New York City it's $116.50 per month. How much was that car payment again? We'll pause here for dramatic effect…

OK, if you're determined that you simply must own a car

and are willing to accept the financial consequences, then how much will you spend? If you pay cash, at least you will have no additional interest expense. Do you need a new car? Maybe used is OK? Special rims? Special paint? Is the upgraded sound system really worth making payments to get? At least, try for a cash purchase.

We have nothing against the stylish rims and paint jobs we see out there. Many look pretty sharp. We just hope they're paid in full. If there is any debt attached to them, they get ugly really fast. They are not helping anyone get from point A to point B any better than the car would without them. Same is true for the upgraded stereo. Why would we pay interest expense for any of these things? It's transportation, nothing more. Give us the economy car, one should be enough, and a couple of bicycles.

Time for our reality check. We realize people have all kinds of complicated emotions tied up in their cars. A big industry has spent fortunes to create these emotions. We probably won't convince everyone to make their smartest financial decisions when it comes to buying a car. But maybe just a little improvement?

Remember our mission: we'd just like to make the world a little less stupid. Go ahead and waste some money on a car if you must. But maybe you won't buy the 10 speaker sound system, maybe the standard 5 speakers will be enough? Maybe standard rims look good enough? *There Will Be Math*. The average length of car loan at this writing is well over 60 months. If we convince people to reduce their payment just $10 per month, we just saved over $600 per reader. A little less stupid world. Mission accomplished.

The DontBeStupid.club Summary:

- Car payments are just another kind of debt. Their impact is greater because they are relatively large payments and continue for a long time period.

- Not everyone really needs a car.

- Enormous amounts of advertising have conditioned us since birth that we must buy cars we cannot really afford. Breaking this emotional conditioning is difficult.

- Spending a little less on a car will help. Try to limit any car purchase to just what is needed.

9.
Student Loans

THE AVERAGE STUDENT loan debt for a student in the USA graduating with a Bachelor degree in 2015? $35,000. It gets worse. Average student loan for an MBA graduating in 2015? $100,000. The interest alone is going to cost at least another $50,000 before that's paid off. According to the Federal Reserve, total student loan debt in the USA stands at about $1.27 trillion. And that figure is too low. It doesn't include the credit card debt. Students borrow a lot of money to get through school.

Follow the Money. Lenders profit. And the very BIG BUSINESS of higher education profits. And the bill is paid by... wait for it.... STUDENTS!!

Yes, screw the people in the process of learning, because in a few more years they'll be too smart to do this! Let's hook kids on the debt drugs before they know how bad debt is for them. And sell it to them under the guise of helping them get the education they desperately need to get ahead in the world. Great business plan. And total Bullshit.

Student loans are the single biggest government subsidy of any industry in the USA. Without the government subsidy, the price of school would become efficient. Supply and demand might actually be allowed to set the prices. Without government subsidy, the price of a college degree would drop to a fraction of what it costs today. Who knows, maybe degrees would actually be priced at what they're really worth in the job market.

But no one cares about all that pricing efficiency stuff. The profits on student debt can be maintained as long as there are enough students who will take on the debt before getting smart enough to avoid it. Just keep driving up the demand and don't control the prices. Brilliant idea. Only politicians could come up with that one.

In the USA, there are very few debts that survive a bankruptcy. There are only three that effect the typical citizen: debts to the IRS, child support, and student loans. What the hell are student loans doing on that list? Taxes not paid and taking care of your kids, those seem especially important. But student loans? Declare bankruptcy and your car loan is gone, credit card debts gone, medical bills gone. They may have even saved your life but their bill is gone in bankruptcy.

But student loans? They're with you until you die. Why is that? *Follow the Money*. Once students understand the game, there would be mass bankruptcy filings if these loans could be discharged. People want their money back. But there will be no refunds on this screwing.

We'll admit it. We're impassioned about Student Loans. Here's our dream scenario; everyone gets together and then doesn't pay. That would work, by the way, but it won't happen. It's a beautiful scenario too... Who would suffer? Overpriced colleges and profiteering banks. Only the guilty would be punished for what is obviously their crime. Maybe a few politicians too. Beautiful thought.

Maybe it's not as crazy as it sounds. For one thing, if you are truly desperate, try the "undue hardship" route. We are not lawyers and you need some advice here. But with the right judge, you might get a partial or even total discharge. You really do have to be at least a little bit desperate though. It won't work if you just want to drink better wine. But do not believe the myth that there is no way out. If you are truly desperate, it's worth a shot. Statistically, if a lawyer says it's worth a day in court, there's maybe 30% probability of getting at least partial relief. And if you have any medical condition that restricts your earning, then you have a pretty high probability of some relief. Get in there with your best limp.

There are less drastic steps too. We are not doing a handbook on student loans here and cannot go too deep into tactics. But if you have student loan debt, be certain to invest the time in https://studentaid.ed.gov/sa/repay-loans/forgiveness-cancellation to at least become fluent with your government sanctioned options. There is no universal easy answer yet, debt relief for everyone does not exist. But there are a lot of plans "nibbling around the edges" to offer relief to some. Income driven repayment plans, teachers, veterans, public service and non-profit workers, police officers, firefighters, most government employees, there are a lot of specific areas where a little help may be available.

And join activist groups. Stay informed and make some noise. There is growing political pressure for relief. Especially within the Democratic party, there is considerable appetite for student debt relief legislation. And the USA has a long history of peaceful protest eventually succeeding. Make sure the politicians see you and know how you vote.

There is recent precedent for government sanctioned debt write-off too. In response to the mortgage debt crisis in the USA which started in 2008, the Home Affordable Modification Program (HAMP) was put in place. Among other assistances, HAMP and related programs forced banks to accept some debt write-down on mortgages. And "short-sale" became a common term, meaning lenders settled mortgage loans for less than full value.

The student loan crisis is equally as unsustainable as the mortgage crisis. It's really just a matter of time before something pops somewhere. It's not impossible, in fact it's quite probable. Hang in there and delay paying for as long as possible. There were no refunds in the mortgage write-offs. Those who'd paid more on their mortgage before they short-sold their homes did not get any refunds. They just lost more of their money.

For the record, we have no student loan debt. We borrowed no money to go to college. We let the budget tell us what we wanted, and made it work. We're not trying to be annoying or anything, but it's not impossible to get your degree without borrowing. It's not even difficult. But that won't help anyone already graduated and in debt. (see Bonus Content at our website if you want to know more: http://dontbestupid.club/money-bonus-content/)

The DontBeStupid.club Summary:

- Student loans are just another big business preying on the uninformed.

- It's worth looking for any relief specific to your situation.

- Stay informed and politically active. The present course is unsustainable. Relief is probable.

10.
Credit Cards

JUST CALL THEM debt creators.

Let's skip ahead right to *Simplify*. There is only one way a credit card is OK, and that's if you pay the bill in full every month. Pay it in full, collect your rewards, and go merrily on with life. If you do that, congratulations, you might be the only one. If you cannot do that, and that means about 99% of everyone being honest, then get rid of your credit card(s).

You've heard this advice before, many times. But since the average US household has over $15,000 in credit card debt and carries 3.7 cards, obviously hearing it isn't working. Of course, most of what's said about getting rid of credit cards is stupid. And most of it is promoted by the same people who give you the cards. Maybe that's why debt keeps rising?

We'll try and say something more useful, and a little less stupid. The next things we say will be different from what you've heard before.

If you are carrying credit card debt, do this. Today. Start using your debit card instead. Use only your debit card. Buy only what you can afford to pay for right now, in real time. Pay-as-you-go. Bury all your credit cards deep in a drawer. Forget they exist.

The reason you don't burn the credit cards is you might have to grab one in an emergency. No, you do not need to put 6 months' cash in a savings account as your emergency fund. You hear that crap all the time. It's bad advice. *Think for Yourself.* Ignore it. What you need is a way to pay for an emergency if one happens. Available credit on a card works just fine. And a few months of payments without new charges will start making plenty of room on your credit card to pay for an emergency.

An added bonus of using a credit card for an emergency? If you have to declare bankruptcy due to your emergency, you don't pay off the card. If you feel bad, you can tell MasterCard you're sorry later. But they can afford it while you cannot right now.

And we advise you not to feel sorry for Mr. MasterCard. He's gotten very rich by helping people spend more than they should. The constant programming to spend needs to have some consequences. We'd like to see all the perpetrators suffer a lot more, but we'll settle for people charging their emergencies and wiping it out in a bankruptcy if their need is great enough. The world gets a little less stupid every time that happens.

So right now today, stop using credit cards for daily spending. Start using your debit card and buy only what you have money to pay for. And start thinking of credit cards as your emergency fund. Ignore them, except to grab them on your way to get a root canal.

Just start treating your old credit card bills the same as any other monthly bill and pay the minimum. Absorb them into your monthly budget cycle. Think of them as part of your rent or mortgage. Use money you have allocated to the categories for Investing to cover the minimum payments. If you have to tap into the Luxuries category, then do that too. We're just getting started here and this is not the whole answer. We just need to get a pay-as-you-go rhythm going here. When getting started on a debt-free lifestyle, this is not the time to worry about paying extra on your cards or paying down the highest interest one first, etc.

Don't Be Distracted. Anything that distracts you from the main objective is a waste of time. Start by just getting in the habit of paying as you go. No new debt purchases. That's all we care about right now. Breaking the habit, getting off the debt drug. The very first goal is to get comfortable leading a pay-as-you-go life. The old credit card bills are now just a monthly bill, part of the rent or mortgage, and a painful reminder of a past life when you were programmed to spend more money than you had.

The pay-down on your credit cards will come later, from money you will set aside to invest, but only when it's time to invest. When you do get into the financial position where investing make sense, then there will be nothing else in the investment universe that can compete with the returns for paying off those credit cards. But remember from this point onward, paying off those cards is an investment and must not be prioritized in your spending any higher than that.

Most people tell you something different. *Follow the Money.* It is in everyone else's best interest to have you prioritize your credit cards so highly. Everyone else, but not you. Making sure you pay your credit card debt is their top priority. But here's the bottom line. Keep your options open. Credit card debt is wiped out in a bankruptcy. And filing for bankruptcy is sometimes the correct financial strategy. *Think for Yourself*. After you clear away all the emotion, alleged social stigma etc., the only thing really worthy of critical thinking is the money. The economics of the situation are all that matter, not what anyone else thinks. *Don't Be Distracted*. Make the best financial choice here and ignore all the emotions.

Bankruptcy is frequently a smart move. In our experience, only about 1 of every 3 who should choose this course actually do it. And we only talk to people smart enough to consider the choice. We think a lot more people should be considering it. But there are a lot of stupid people out there just ignoring their best option.

There Will Be Math. If your credit card debt is high enough, or you have additional debt like medical bills or car loans, or whatever debt situation you are in, if your budget can never get you to the point of investing, then you are better off just not paying off the debts. Your credit score isn't worth that much money. Just file bankruptcy and wipe out the debts. The time you spend with a lower credit score will not cost you nearly as much real money as paying off the debts. Plus, you also get the immediate stress relief of instantly owing no money to anyone.

In fact, if you follow our advice and are committed to never borrow again, then the lower credit score will make no meaningful difference in your life whatsoever. The bankruptcy filing just wipes out the debts and you continue on with your pay-as-you-go lifestyle, but now it's also debt free.

And here's some stupidity masquerading as irony. Even if you want to be stupid and borrow again, you will build up a decent enough credit score faster after a bankruptcy than you could have by juggling and paying off the debts. If you remain debt-free and pay your bills on time, your credit score 5 years later can easily be over 700. It likely would not be that high if you're still juggling today's debts, and definitely won't be that high if juggling the debts causes you to make some late payments.

Among the many, many famous people to declare bankruptcy, we have three favorites: Walt Disney, Henry Ford, and Abraham Lincoln. Isn't that a list of USA royalty? Yes, it is. And it's also a list of people who were bankrupt. Mr. Ford filed twice. *Think for Yourself.* If it was OK for them, why the hell shouldn't you do it? Make your best financial decision here and tell everyone else to mind their own business. And please know that the moral outrage is driven by propaganda from the debt holders.

Emotional opinions are worthless. If you have to humor some people, just tell them you wish it could have been different. They'll all be jealous when you're buying them lunch for cash anyway. And if you feel guilty, run for President afterwards. You're probably better qualified for the job now.

The credit card discussion is very simple. Credit cards are poison, just like a drug and addictive. Stop using credit cards. Get accustomed to pay-as-you-go living. And then either pay off the cards as your first investment, or declare bankruptcy and get rid of the debts all at once.

We are going to spend absolutely zero time on choosing the "best" card, or how to get the most rewards, or surfing for free cash, or extended warranties, or fraud protection, or any other marketing BS designed to hook you on the credit drug. Can the trivial value in any or all of those possibly be worth it? Why carry such an addictive debt creator in your pocket? Do you want some free samples of heroin? We pay cash for our plane tickets. We didn't charge $30K on a credit card just to get enough points.

Simplify. Do not use credit cards. Ignore all the noise surrounding them. There are better uses for your time. And they wouldn't put all those bells and whistles on them if using the card was such a great idea for you in the first place. Just lipstick on a pig.

The DontBeStupid.club summary:

- Credit cards are just debt creators.

- Step one is to stop using credit cards and practice pay-as-you-go.

- Credit cards are to be prioritized and paid down only as an investment choice.

- If it's impossible to invest, then bankruptcy is an option that deserves serious consideration.

- The best credit card is NO credit card. Debt-free people don't need the "points".

11.
Saving

LET'S SPEND A few minutes to distinguish saving from investing.

Define the Target. Saving – Protecting from destruction or damage. It follows that saving money is about protecting it from destructions (like spending it on wine!).

Saving is accumulating some money safely for a future need or needs. Saving money is not investing. Saving is about preservation, not growing. *Don't Be Distracted.* An extra percent interest on a savings account is not worth the effort to switch banks opening the account. Accumulation in savings comes from what you deposit into an account. Any return at all is just a small bonus. Convenience is at least as important, and usually more important.

Saving is a short term goal. You save for the vacation next summer. Or you save up for a car. You might even save up the down payment for a house (as long as you're not stupid about it). In all cases, you are far more concerned about safety than anything else.

Saving is money you set aside and plan to spend sometime in the not too distant future. Or, maybe you even plan to save it forever. But saving is not investing. Do not confuse the terms in your head. *Don't Be*

Distracted. The world of investing likes to use the word "saving" a lot, and they like to attach it to their products. Saving sounds like something you "should" do, so it makes selling you an investment easier. And saving sounds safe. It sounds better to say you are saving for retirement than to say you're betting the S&P 500 index will go up over the next 10 years.

If you want to really save for something, you must pick a zero risk method. A savings account or CD is a good idea, and you don't need to care much about the interest rate. You care about safety and convenience. The shorter the timeline the less difference is made by any interest rate differences. And do not take any risk at all unless you are perfectly able to get less money back than you "saved".

Saving a little money is a worthwhile pursuit. We highly recommend having a little cash in the bank before proceeding to investing. There is something very reassuring about knowing you can take $500 out of an ATM just because you want to and it's no big deal.

The DontBeStupid.club Summary:

- Saving is about safety first and always.

- Saving is not about getting high returns. The accumulation comes from what you put in.

- Some saving is a good idea. It's just a nice feeling to have a little cash in the bank.

12.
Investing

OUTSTANDING. WE'RE PAYING the rent and eating without fear of the bills, we have no debt, and we're ready for the next step.

At this point, we hope you are thinking "investing, wow it was hard to get here". Right on! Now you know there are many better uses for your money than stocks and bonds, etc. Everything that comes before this chapter is a better "investment". No car loans? No credit card debt? Happy where you live? OK, please continue...

If you get to this point, meaning you really do have some extra money looking to "go to work", then congratulations. You have accomplished quite a lot already. Just by getting here, you are way ahead of most "investors". Seriously, look in the mirror and take a bow.

OK, so now we are ready to be an investor. Finally, we are ready to pay some fees.

Oops, that may have sounded a little cynical, but that is an important realization. You have to pay to play. There is no shortage of investment products and sellers out there, all of them competing for your business, and to collect the fees from you. Their paychecks depend on it.

Do not ever be confused. "Investing" is an industry

driven by salespeople chasing their paycheck. There is nothing wrong with that, but it's important to understand the investment marketplace is no different than any other place where people try to sell you something. Their paycheck depends on you buying. Like any market, some are better, more ethical people than others. But all of them work hard to get you buying and the industry has had many decades to work on its bullshit.

Do you know the term for a 10% drop in the stock market? It's called a "correction". If you think that sounds stupid, you're way ahead of anyone saying it on TV with a straight face. If you "invested" before the decline, it does not feel like a correction, right? It feels like you lost 10%. And you are right!

You know who names a 10% loss a "correction"? The people selling the investment to you. *Don't Be Distracted.* This is just another case of using a name to confuse the buyer. Nothing has been corrected. We just lost 10%. There is nothing correct about losing 10%.

Do you know what losing 20% is called? It's called a Bear. We like bears. Bears are cool. Why is losing 20% called a "bear"? Well, there are several good stories about that, but here's the bottom line. Calling it a "massive loss" won't generate any fees, will it? Doesn't "Bear" sound better? Plus, you feel cool using this lingo too. We lost 20% but we call it something cool. We were caught in the Bear market.

The barrage of ideas, sales pitches and misleading terms for "investing" your money is truly astonishing. And as we've said before, wherever you bleed money, the world hangs a bucket. It's all set up so you can never run out of choices for how to pay someone a fee to "help" you with your money. It's an all-you-can-eat buffet of fee-generating investment choices.

When you see all these choices, don't feel overwhelmed. *Simplify.* Most of them are just stupid. No one really needs all the food on that buffet. Save your money, you just don't need all those choices.

Instead of looking at the products available, you start with your own needs. Your goals guide your investments, not the other way around. Again, *Simplify.* There are really only two questions worth considering when investing. What do we want from this investment? How much risk are we willing to take? Knowing those two answers, and then making the best choice available, that's all there is to investing. Really, that's all there is to it. Don't ever let it be more complicated.

Now, the products are usually made more complicated than necessary, the sales materials are as persuasive as legally possible, and the true costs are well hidden. This all adds up to making the evaluation a little harder, but as long as we remain focused on cutting through all the clutter and getting to the answer we want, then investing is never difficult.

At this point, you are ready to choose between many possible courses based on your own priorities. And unfortunately, at this point we can't be as helpful as we'd like. Everyone's situation is unique and there is no "one size fits all" plan. But there are some pitfalls you can avoid no matter what course you choose. We can offer some universal guidance here.

There Will Be Math. But good news. It's just simple arithmetic. We're talking grade school level stuff here. The most complex financial data you can find can be simplified to a series of A+B =C statements, and a little division to get percentages. Well, maybe there will be some subtraction in there too. Like during a "correction".

All of those graphs and derivatives, EPS and EBITDAs, ratios and ROIs, on and on, all that expensive sounding lingo, it's just arithmetic. The added complications are there mostly to impress you and convince you that higher fees are worth paying. It's pseudoscience.

OK, we will allow that between experts sometimes it's more convenient to communicate with more complex statements. Physicists discussing string theory together can do it more efficiently than if required to make sure we all understand it along with them.

Like physicists with string theory, financial professionals may find some efficiency in discussing Bollinger Bands. Who knows, they may even get aroused talking about their relationship with Keltner Channels. Lucky them. But who else needs it? All of investing can be reduced to simple terms. The only thing stopping that is fear the "professional" advice won't be worth as much in fees if discussed simply.

We're only insulting the people selling to us that way, trying to appear smart when in reality it's all a bluff. If a financial pro ever addresses you with terms you don't understand, just require them to *Simplify*. Refuse to buy their product unless you completely understand it. There is nothing, repeat NOTHING, too complicated to explain in simple terms. They'll either *Simplify* very quickly, or realize you are not stupid and move on to an easier sales target. They may even call you stupid, which of course is the ultimate in irony. (Remember the name calling in our dedication for this book?)

The world of investment choices is fascinating. It's also very large. In fact, part of what makes it fascinating is that something so simple can be turned into its own giant world of stupidity. We have another book about money, "Don't Be Stupid about Investing". It's devoted 100% to the subject of investing. In it, we *Simplify* that ridiculously large universe of choices into something far less stupid. But as we hope is becoming clear, there are a lot of other areas where we need to be less stupid first. So, let's get back to this money book...

We regret there is no truly useful "one size fits all" investing plan that we can write here. But if you follow just the advice given in this chapter, along with all the other best uses of your money before getting here, then you cannot go too far off target. As long as you remember it's a sales game, just like when the car salesman says "can I help you". If you listen with that same level of skepticism, you cannot get too much wrong.

Although we cannot offer a "one size fits all" plan, we can offer one piece of universal advice. The single biggest piece of advice the truly wealthy pass on to their heirs? **Never Risk Principal.**

There are no called third strikes in the world of investing. There is no urgency to swing. Any urgency is usually coming from the sales efforts trying to get you to buy. It's really ok to miss an investment opportunity. Even miss a lot of them. No big deal. There will be more chances, and you still have your money to invest later when you are more certain.

But if you make a mistake, your money is gone. You are out of the game. Survival is far more important than scoring at every opportunity. **Never Risk Principal**.

The DontBeStupid.club summary:

- There are many better uses for your money before getting into the more traditional world of investing.

- Investing is primarily about choosing between products you pay for. And the sales pitches are extreme.

- The terminology of investing distracts from the underlying concepts which are simple, and not worth much in fees.

- No single answer is the right investment for everyone. "Don't Be Stupid about Investing" is devoted 100% to investing and goes into greater detail.

- If in doubt, Never Risk Principal.

13.
Charity

EVERYONE'S FAVORITE. It makes us feel good. We gave money to a worthy cause. Aren't we special?

First Things First. We can only be as charitable as we can afford to be. We are not ready to prioritize charity until the money is truly available. You cannot carry debt and give to charity at the same time, for example. It is more charitable to get richer first and then give more to charity later.

If you want to be charitable and don't have extra money, donate time instead. That makes you very special. And if you donate money you don't really have? That makes you stupid.

So now we're ready to donate.

Really caring about our fellow human is surprisingly rare. And now we know there's no such thing as a "good" tax deduction (see chapter on Home debt). So that is not the reason for our charity, right? We really must care! But *Open Mind.* Sorry to say, too frequently we are being stupid with our charitable contributions.

Follow the Money. Unfortunately, charity is a big business. Some of these businesses "make" a lot of money. But we can make sure our charity helps the people we wanted to help and not the middleman. We

76

do this by not being stupid.

Charities are rated by different agencies. These "watchdogs" have different levels of credibility, and some are better than others. All probably provide some rating benefit. But you have to be careful of the motivations. Frequently they have an agenda and just want to convince you their favorites are better than others.

Simplify. There is one evaluation we like above all others. The audited financial statements and form 990 filed with the IRS by the charity itself. Among other things, the 990 discloses the salaries of the highest paid executives. Almost without exception, the charities supporting high salaries are a bad idea.

If you really believe in charity, then you won't be commanding the salary of a CEO at regular "for profit" corporations. Too frequently we see this idea that you have to pay competitively to get top talent. That sounds logical, but it's bullshit. That argument is made by the people who want to collect those top salaries. It is not an argument made by charitable people. Plenty of qualified people will do those jobs for half the salary. City of Hope, American Cancer Society, American Heart Association... really, those salaries don't look too charitable to us. US Olympic Committee? Yeah, that's supposedly a charity too. You'd love 25% of those salaries.

Salaries are not linear. At some point, you have more than you need and spend the rest on luxury. Exactly how charitable can you be if you need a million-dollar salary to work for a charity? Would you eat poorly making only

$250,000 per year? Maybe you could donate the other $750,000 to your charity? Just a suggestion...

Anyway, call us crazy, but we like to donate to charities where the people working there make salaries that look a little more charitable. We like the form 990. It gives us some quick and easy answers.

You know what qualifies as a "highly efficient" charity by most of the "watchdogs"? 80% of donations getting through to the intended target. Some "watchdogs" will tell you 75% is great.

Exxon Mobile has an administrative burden of a little over 3%. That may not be a totally fair comparison. After all, the charity biz is different from the energy biz. But 20% burden is highly efficient? Really? Hard to see how that can qualify as "highly efficient". Much of the private sector would consider it terrible.

Follow the Money. There is no real logic to the grade of "highly efficient". We call this placing the target after the arrow lands. They show you a target already hit, and tell you it's a bullseye. It's like getting to grade yourself in school. A lot more A's are given out that way. Watchdog agencies might mean well, but they'd be out of business if they called too many charities "inefficient". So they grade on a curve, and the curve would be mostly failures if they had to compete in the "for profit" world.

There really are some charities out there with ratings in the mid to upper nineties for their efficiency. Just like Exxon. We don't want to endorse any one charity, but we suggest that looking for this type of truly well-run charity is a little less stupid than donating to anyone just rated "efficient".

Most charities begging for your money are also begging to keep their infrastructure going. They're not bad people. In fact, they usually support worthy causes. It's just that there are better choices for our charity dollar. If the world is a little less stupid, maybe the worst ones will go out of business.

Religions and churches are a specific kind of organized charity. Maybe your church is important enough that you don't mind staying in debt while donating. As long as that's a decision you put some critical thought into, then maybe it's a good decision. But if it's driven by emotion, then it's stupid. Specifically, guilt. Religions use guilt to extract money the same way other products use sex appeal. Same tactic, different emotion.

Follow the Money. Religions get most of their money from donations. And they make one hell of a sales pitch to keep it going. If you have extra money and want to support your church, great. But if you have to stress out over rent or groceries, then donating is just stupid. And we have a serious problem with putting guilt on people to make donations they cannot afford. That is pure evil, not something you want in a church.

Many religions use bible passages to support a notion of "10% to God". That's stupid. There are an equal or greater number of passages saying something different. *There Will Be Math.* A fixed percentage of an unknown amount is stupid. For some people, 10% of their money is just part of what they'd spend on luxuries. Great. They can give "10% to God" and we don't even mind if you make them feel guilty.

But we all know people tithing who cannot afford their groceries. And that's stupid. We doubt any deity worthy of worship ever suggested such an idea. That's a business decision made by people who don't really care about you. *Think for Yourself*. Do not ever donate because of guilt.

Here's a 100% efficient way to be charitable. Look online for your nearest women's shelter. They probably post a "needs list". You will find they usually need things like toilet paper and non-perishable food. Go buy $100 worth of what they need. Drop it off. And then feel special, 100% NOT stupid.

The DontBeStupid.club summary:

- True charity is rare. The world would be a little less stupid with more of it.

- Organized charities have expenses and not all your donation gets to the intended cause. These are worth review to make sure you're not supporting high salaries.

- Churches are a specific category of organized charities. Donate accordingly.

14.
Final Thoughts

WE KNOW MOST of these topics sounded familiar. Most people "kind of" understand them. But stupidity happens in the gap between "kind of" and "real" understanding. For example, we're sure plenty of people "kind of" understood money when they signed their student loan documents. But many would have made different choices if they had a "real" understanding.

If we did our job, then now you know too much about money to ever be stupid again. Or at least you know when you're choosing to be stupid, so someone else is not just taking advantage of all the prior programming.

You now know that money is many different things, and the names are used to distract us. Money is really just worth what you can buy with it, and nothing else. You know tomorrow's dollar will be something different than today.

As soon as you leave these pages, you again will be barraged with information designed to make you think Money is a complicated subject. This is always an attempt to take your money. *Don't Be Distracted.* Remain clear in applying our principles and money will always be simple.

There Will Be Math. You cannot escape the fact that

money requires a little math. But it's simple math, mostly just addition and subtraction. Do it and you can't be stupid.

And you now know that Debt is the most insidious drug ever forced on a population. You are hooked before you know any better. And getting clean takes some effort. But the rewards are worth every step of progress.

You now have the "real" understanding that home payments and car payments are the two biggest debt decisions you will make, and reducing these even a little will have the most significant effects on the rest of your life. Getting them right is the foundation of a successful money management strategy. And you know to not let anyone else tell you how much to spend.

We know much of what we suggest is not exactly what the mainstream says is right. Too bad. We're proud of that. They're the ones who created this debt machine and dropped successor generations into it without giving them the chance to fight back. Critical thinking is the enemy of the debt machine. And we don't care who's feathers get ruffled. Maybe we can put them all out of a job.

Money is a big issue, perhaps the biggest area of stupidity in the world, and we know we didn't cover it all. We didn't get into 401k's, employer matches or many other topics commonly encountered in daily life. They're all specific to investing, and we get into all of that in our book "Don't Be Stupid about Investing".

If you have another area we should have included, please let us know. We hope there are more "Money Books" in our future. It's a subject where stupidity does too much damage.

We've tried to keep it entertaining while informing on a subject where a lot of stupidity exists. We never intend to make light of an important subject. But money should never be so important that we cannot laugh about it. We've all been stupid with money, and what else can you do but laugh about it? But it's more fun to laugh at the people trying to take our money.

Stupidity costs us. Time, anxiety, cash, and frequently pain and suffering too. Stupidity is BIG business. And never forget, everywhere we are stupid, someone else is collecting the payoff. They work hard to keep you stupid.

We hope we made just a few dollars' difference here. Just a few dollars less stupidity for enough people, and we've succeeded in our mission to make the world a little less stupid.

Applying the DontBeStupid.club critical thought principles finds answers. Answers are the cure for stupidity.

Hopefully we are all a little less stupid about money.

15.
Don't Be Stupid Club

At DontBeStupid.club we make the world a little less stupid.

We do not take a position on an issue until we've thought about it critically. We always start with an *Open Mind*. We just apply our principles and think about the question. A little critical thinking is all that's required to quickly reach most answers. Sometimes a little more work is required. But we always get to the answer.

We don't care what people think. But we do care about how they think. Any well-reasoned opinion deserves respect. And opinions without basis are just stupid. Differing answers are fine. All we want is to make the world a little less stupid. If you hate our answer and have a well-reasoned opposition, GREAT!

We're all in this adventure together. We're stupid too. We are all conditioned from birth to think the wrong way. But we are a little less stupid for trying to fix that.

Critical thinking is a skill that can be learned. It's not even a difficult skill. It's harder to be a good welder or good coder or good baseball player. It's impossible for most of us to dunk a basketball. But we all can be good thinkers.

Critical thinking is a way of looking at the world. It's a

framework for thinking about anything. You're going to spend time thinking anyway, why not make the most of it? We think life is easier this way. You never feel lost if you know how to think.

Most disagreements we observe just come from people being stupid. Arguing points without defining their targets... adding complexity to hide their own inadequacies... trying to lie their way to a profit... going against nature... doing the wrong things first... all just stupid.

The world can be a much better place if we are all a little less stupid.

And know this. If you apply our critical thinking principles, then you can never be stupid. The stupidity is all around you, but it can never get YOU! Critical thinking is stronger than stupidity. Answers always equal power.

Our goal is to make a little difference in your life and entertain. Let us know how we did. We'd love to hear from you.

Visit http://DontBeStupid.club if you'd like more.

Our Amazon Store is located at: http://astore.amazon.com/dontbclub-20. It's where you'll find some of the products we like. Nothing in our store is stupid. You don't pay anything extra, but we get a little commission if you buy here. And we appreciate it. It helps us keep making the world a little less stupid.

We thank you for the time you spent with us.